FAIR DAY IN AN ANCIENT TOWN

The Mineral Point Poetry Series

MINERAL POINT POETRY SERIES   NO. 3

Kiki Petrosino, Editor

FAIR DAY IN AN ANCIENT TOWN poems

Greg Allendorf

Brain Mill Press · Green Bay, Wisconsin

Copyright © 2016 by Greg Allendorf. All rights reserved.

Published in the United States by Brain Mill Press.
ISBN 978-1-942083-22-1

Cover photograph © Barbara Diener.
Cover design by Stray King Design.
Interior illustration by Ann O'Connell.
Interior design by Williams Writing, Editing & Design.

www.brainmillpress.com

The Mineral Point Poetry Series, number 3.

Published by Brain Mill Press, the Mineral Point Series is
edited by Kiki Petrosino. In odd years, the series invites
submissions of poetry chapbooks around a theme. In even
years, the editor chooses a full collection.

for Matthew

Contents

Foreword

In Sonnet 31, Shakespeare illustrates his all-consuming love for the young man by turning him into a small universe. "Thy bosom is endearèd with all hearts / Which I, by lacking, have supposèd dead," the poet claims. In this sonnet's formulation of eros, the young man represents all the promise of future delight, but it's irrevocably mixed with the poet's remembered sorrow over departed or failed relationships. "Thou art the grave where buried love doth live," Shakespeare declares, "hung with the trophies of my lovers gone." The poem argues that true love can revive the joys and hurts of the seemingly dead past, making green an emotional landscape that despair had once depleted.

But the process of coming to life through love is painful. In Greg Allendorf's *Fair Day in an Ancient Town*, the speaker and his beloved are, by turns, passionately bonded and viciously feuding. Like Shakespeare's young man, the beauty of the beloved incites ecstasy and sorrow in the speaker: "O my love and his ungrateful smile, / O my love who glares out of the trees; / whose beauty forced me through the lavender" ("Shepherd's Song"). Despite the contentious nature of the relationship between these two lovers, the landscape and the body of the beloved remain erotically fused: "The pasture seems an echo of his thighs" ("The Good Shepherd").

It's no accident that these poems are conversant with the pastoral tradition of Western poetry, as they imagine idealized rural landscapes as sites for (sometimes dangerous) love play. Allendorf's poems are a kind of dark mirror reflecting on canonical pastorals like Christopher Marlowe's "The Passionate Shepherd to His Love," in which the lovestruck speaker offers a proliferation of future-tense promises to the object of his adoration:

> And I will make thee beds of roses
> And a thousand fragrant posies,
> A cap of flowers, and a kirtle
> Embroidered all with leaves of myrtle

Allendorf's speaker makes promises, too. But whereas Marlowe's shepherd appears to speak from a "real-time" moment of active seduction, we get the impression that the speaker of *Fair Day* is contemplating his relationship postfall. The wooing words that we encounter in poems like "We Will Become One in Luxor" capitalize on the future tense as a means to highlight the poignancy of the speaker's plaint. "Luxor" emerges as an already lost landscape, the "ancient town" where "buried love doth live." What is promised there is a fantasy of "oneness" that, the speaker knows, cannot be achieved in this lifetime:

> For love to thrive
> in us can only prove that we're alive
> in Luxor.   How our tomb walls then will swell
> like glass   and blow like sugar   through our hands.
> I will   see you.
> I will see you there in Luxor.

Unlike Shakespeare's young man, the beloved of *Fair Day* is not just a passive vessel for the speaker's poetic fantasies. Throughout these poems, the beloved is dynamically active, moving with and against the speaker's efforts to fix him in time. In reading these poems, we can't dismiss the power and preternatural ubiquity of the beloved; parts of his body appear in the landscape as surreal blazons. Consider the otherworldly transformation that occurs in "Massage":

> He drags a boundless energy
> through the web of muscles.
> Like a crane
> possessed by grace,   the double S
>   of his hands, a fluid massacre
> of stillness.

Fluidity and stillness. Grace and massacres. Allendorf's poems traffic in these ardent contradictions. The speaker grieves for the irretrievable past even as he recognizes how loneliness has brought a dark vitality to his utterances. For Allendorf, the hands of the beloved are, simultaneously, instruments of pain and deliverers of grace. Just so, the poems of *Fair Day in an Ancient Town* are for anyone who has struggled to resolve the crisis of heartbreak through art. Allendorf teaches us that whole worlds of creative action lie on the other side of loss. In "Catamount," Allendorf presents an image of the speaker and his beloved as a single taxidermied wildcat, a once-living organism that must, in death, be split in order to become art. This unique metaphor illustrates the necessary transformation of the artist from grieving lover to luminous maker:

> I hate couplets, I hate couples, hate
> the tension our avulsion can create.
>
> Break the halves and bang
>   them each apart

at the pearly lips.   Whenas the heart's
        concerned, I'd rather be alone:
a skin stretched over plastic without bone.

Kiki Petrosino
Editor, Mineral Point Poetry Series

FAIR DAY IN AN ANCIENT TOWN

Nota

I did the love and dressed for my scant part
in the love. As I escape my cheap
dress shirt, crystal flies embellish me.
Make of my blue aura a dark mark,
like a laurelled editor would make.
Save me from the fact of punctuation.
It daubs a deeper blue over the wrist,
arrests the jaw beneath a wet stop sign;
I wade through the weeds and swing my arms.
Block the end-stop's blow and delude me
into yet another glass-winged paragraph.
I imagine clouds of rich cologne
distend the walls of your pale blue estate.
I invent this written history,
commemorate our sordid run,
and dive into the pool with open mouth
and lungs indifferent.   At least I loved.

Cri de Coeur

I fear the three old heaving orgasms
of Eurydice persist in me. I've returned
my mail to sender, put my hairless dog

out into the field of mauve and piss-
tinted amaryllis.   Saguaros howl
owls from their adoring little mouths.

I fear three years of death inside myself.
        I take my injured man inside myself,
crushed like velvet under a half-set moon.

Null-set,   boneset,   ague-weed,   old rune
        that snips a scientific tendon.   Loons
        love sometimes, when they cannot collapse.

I drag my tongue up through his ancient mane.

        I list to hold him and he is the moon.
I feel my way through bracken in the dark

way a tipped astronomer gets drunk
and body-lusty laid out on the plank.
He fits me with a shunt and lets a finch

move into my side-meat.   Inch by inch,
the moon unspools its worth from its white hole.
        I drool over my paint-by-number soul.

Sober

Never so great the shiftlessness. The rest
of the night, I'll stare into the wall
and think a poem about alcohol.
I'll write about the luxury that's failed
me so far this month. It's April now,
and still no desperate gift of unreturned
yearning. Usually, I'm writing reams
of crushy ones each day. Lush, bitter birds
that soar into the window one by one.
I just can't muster it. They hurt me some,
the poems and their people, all the pearl
of torture. I confess: I am afraid;
It's hard to sleep without a tiny veil
of pain to puff with breath and call a sail.

Massage

Lethe. Early morning. Skipping stones
      that bounce along forever and forget
to stop.
             He drags a boundless energy
through the web of muscles.
                Like a crane
possessed by grace,   the double S
      of his hands, a fluid massacre
of stillness.
         An anaphora of moans
and arches—and the endlessness of it.
The way he sews the whole day through, a green
      benediction.
         O, that feels so good,
     my forehead is a lens of porcelain.
I giggle bits of satin.   His ocean
of an arm obscures my brain's blank shore.
     Lethe.
         Afternoon.
             I lie awake,
and every dream resumes its first long sleep.

He moves over my back like an unarmed
        soldier holds his wife before he leaves.
      My mind's
    a candied waterfall
in semigloss, which has forever stopped
      my body.
                  I gulp a length of green
broth and my wet mind becomes a steam.

The Presentation

This is my lordosis: look: my part.

It wants to feel the syllables your heart

putters.   I want your obsessive pulse

     to part with mine only when universe

and starlight disentangle.   Dumb stud, come;

     I'll be the radiator and the heat

it hisses.   I'll paint the memory

 of you on my closed coffin lid and lard

my arteries with your untamed beauty.

     I've assumed the posture of a rapt

ocelot: I moan my smell to you:

swell with me: boil with me: glue

 your sternum to my sternum and we'll do

     what blue jays do until Orion snaps.

Cloying Radiance

Chrysanthemums are cultured pearls are lambs.
You know the round secret rolled
about itself,   hermetic millipede.
You know how to make the udders bleed
calcium and whole vitamin D.

Serotonin's melatonin's speed.
The shepherds on the cloth, the field of gold
in linden leaves enmeshed.   Your candied yam,
your phial of bright toucan feathers yield
a philter *sans* rejoinder.   I fear

Love's a white chrysanthemum with near
one million petals, each an intact tongue.
Slit the seraphs' bellies one by one;
harvest those wild opals once a year.

Good Shepherds

I a shepherd come upon the shepherd as
he bathes and startle him, and startle his green eyes.
The pasture seems an echo of his thighs,
from which ripples every blurry bloom.
I assail him with a sword lily.
I give him a paper gift bag plump with mint-
green M&M'S and Jordan almonds, flint
tools to flay and stuff my heaving trunk.
We drink whatever they drank when the world
smelled only of moss.   We touch and touch
the nature everybody loves so much
to miss.   We piss into the thunderhead.
Hammered and twice amorous, we smudge
our bodies deep with much dark candle-black.
We gallop through the meadow and we graze
on buttercups. We name each other James
and James,   are almost true identicals.
I root for truffles while he clasps a duck's
neck in his tough mouth. I scribble runes
and sound them out with him in the lean-to.
I leave the shepherd home on bingo night,
and he drinks until he's almost literate,
and only a little less beautiful,
and willing only when I will he would.

We Will Become One in Luxor

I will love you.
We will go to Luxor.
We will go to Luxor and we'll lie
with one another there over the miles
of desert.
Of desert we will sup.   We will cup
each other's chins and breasts and we will burn
like fat-cells.   And, like fat-cells,   we will flood
each other's limbs and livers.   With our love
will come a flood of fluids and of clouds.
I will ride you.
I will ride you through Luxor deserts.
I will ride you
and I'll love you   and we'll live
in Luxor on some twelve square feet of sand.
That's how much it takes.   For love to thrive
in us can only prove that we're alive
in Luxor.   How our tomb walls then will swell
like glass   and blow like sugar   through our hands.
I will   see you.
I will see you there in Luxor.
I will see you there in Luxor with your jaw
and earlobes.
You will be my creature   and I'll be
your vulture.   I will love you. I will bend
beneath you.   We'll become one,   in the end.

Embellishment upon a Memory of You Eating Blueberries in Your Car

I have a lapful of currants.
I sit in the gray luxury car.

You have moved away from me. As far
as I can tell, you've disappeared.

Awkward and unreachable for years,
I have kept your altar, and its ink

waxes bolder like an herb
dried behind its label in the dark.

This is where my perseverance breaks
like saline under fur,

this drumhead tight
and motionless, still young in its disuse.

I have a pile of letters,
fable-odd, and uniform in strength.

Oranges grow violet molds and stink.
Diagrams curl yellow on the walls.

Years ago, my other version called
your sanity as hammers do,

a pang out of a string.   Folk instruments
glitter in the ruins.   Rain dilutes

the carnal part of me.   My lap is stained.
You cauterize wet berries in a frame.

I yawn in admiration and recede.

Paean

I dreamt that you were not an idiot.
Your lids held the same green stones,

cheeks the same cute bloat.   I lived alone,
spied on you while you loafed on the strand.

I was your submissive
            in some ancient October cracked
open by the tropics.   Palmetto

tigered your fake tan with shadow.   Sand
sugared your wet sunscreen.
                        Great horned owls

        canvased my dark brain with sensate
bass.   We met in crystal sequences;

still, you would not kiss me.   I authored
            panes of deprivation all night long.

I watched as you went walking.   It was sad,
the way your hairless arms swung on and on,

the way your wet breath pumped into the air.
I disappeared,   awake,   and was not there.

                Now I pant into my comforter
                and find my very voice has blown away.

Shepherd's Song

O, my love and his archaic smile
      that shadowed me into the lavender.
And, O, the lamb's ear of his fresh-shorn hair,
      that faintest light it licked into my eyes.
O, the way his mouth confounded me
      and folded on my mouth there in the fold.
And, O, the glory of his hairy arms,
      the way they lit my eyes a little then.
The pasture lit with shivers, and my thighs
      and their great twitches and my chin
and its italic tremors.   Woe, my gut.
         O my love and his ungrateful smile,
O my love who glares out of the trees;
   whose beauty forced me through the lavender,
who lilted huge, dark words   that ruined me.

My Bedroom, the Coop

One affliction, two afflictions, three.
Love nowhere among them. Audible
Above the sound of rushing, there are birds.
There is not a house left to embrace
My conditioned hair or my well-formed
Forehead. I want only to unpack
Chemical on useless chemical,
Starting at the tip, down to the root.

This is where I store my winter boots.
Here, I keep my iron and my gold
Wrapped around one iris and the next.
Salt and sugar in their canisters,
Plain and near opaque. The odd lung out
In a cooler on the cement stoop.

I want only to unpack my vest,
Put the organs out to cool like old
Relatives, to forget they exist.
Of my balled-up manuscripts a dove
Builds a tangled wreck, and from that nest
Cusses me, half-hidden by the black
Square the paper shade cuts in the floor.

Mouths

His mouth is an unopened felony.
Mine's been twice condemned; I open it
and cross canaries' eyes.   I solder strips
                of cold surgical steel across
my lips. I dream about our heaving lungs
enlaced, of feeding breath into his chest.
    That riot pops my every myelin sheath,
        and dopamine unseals my dancing eyes.

    But he will not uncork his precious trove,
        won't fill my head with miserable crimes.
I drag my blanket through the lemon grove
    and hit my bottle.   Tunnel vision drives
me zigzag. I recline and romance asps;
        and, once my eyes are closed,
                his mouth unclasps.

Rays

Today and yesterday,
          I burped in woe.
     I did tree-sap-deep permutations.
Why, while I pressed fresh-laundered, unharmed,
          silver-shouldered blossoms,   did I hum
within, without, and which-way?
                              It's distress.
     It's the knots. They bloom, they bundle up
          my brain's Peruvian gray daffodil
in small, vespine contractions while the sun
blows fathoms of black shadow from the ants.
          I cannot stand the stretching of my sap.
It rules me.   I hear romances. The shrill
          rummaging of lovers bends the grass
below my window sill.   Every moment
               bodies moving, lashed to one
               another while the heavy sun
               absconds to hang and dream
                    of what it's done.

Backing

Now I think this little fire's split
in two; its halves burned separately
for a while. Then their flames flattened
into brittle minnows. Then they tossed
crystal exclamation points. They broke
and molted gaud and did not shed an ash.
                Then I think my little finger split
                        and every fire fell from it, but I
was neither frightened nor amused. On what
                surface but a bone's? What balcony
        but O-mouthed Cyrano's,   interior
                but yours? There is no flame.
But in the bedroom, where the earrings swing
from their screened display-box, there is silk.

Catamount

Once-feared, now dry and glass-eyed and open-
      faced on an oak plaque in my rich den.

I shine you with Armor All and pace
behind the blackened window flanked with lace.

You're my flooded hemisphere. My right
      brain, a-pulse with magnetic delight.

I hate couplets, I hate couples, hate
the tension our avulsion can create.

Break the halves and bang
      them each apart

at the pearly lips.   Whenas the heart's
      concerned, I'd rather be alone:

a skin stretched over plastic without bone.

An Incantation

I've arrived: a basque of leopard pelts,
     hydroponic marijuana, bright
feather earrings from the Amazon
   basin.   I am eager and prepared.
      I've applied the oil everywhere
and glisten like a Turkish wrestler.
   Christopher Columbus let a gold
   wire out and snared his progeny;
         he tore them back
    through several centuries.
   I am not related to those purse-
faced men. I cannot quite discern
where it is I think that I've arrived.
    Probably a party at some dive.
    Probably the bottom of a pool.
French soaps: Linden Lettuce, *Mer du Sud*:
   A phosphorescent agate is the sea.
 I've removed my loin-doily and rings
and placed them in an oak stash-box for you.
    Peppers, lavender, and catnip drop
   their flowers, jaded hypnotists.   I seize
        my crocodile bag and bolt
   upright into the night without a goal.

Choking

Sixty-fourth notes of consciousness glow
and tumble like struck lightning bugs above
a blacked-out wheat field   sixty miles long.
        Hemidemisemiquaver.   Thong
up my ass   and smile on my face.
        Even smiling glow-most won't erase
                the unsubstantial pain I've felt that tests
        the wisdom and sheer acreage of my chest.
While you argue with a square of blue
        corn light all wrapped and fitted over you,
    I lie and wish   I'd come   out someplace else.
I wish I'd been born a diamond.   The whole shelf
        of dark familial books erupts in flame. If only
    I'd awoken with a name
like diamonds pressed against my rubber neck. If only
        I'd stand a chance at fastening to you,
with your inborn grace and unborn mew,
        your catatonic touch-
down on this earth.   You move so much
        I miss you.

Come the fungus harvest,

                I am a scavenger.

I promenade in a dark locker room.

       I pop my hip and boom through a dark flute

until you pass me,

           then I gape out,

                  mute.

Vogue

Marabou my collar,   death the stalk
of spine taped on my back's arc.   The inane
      river that salts my un-rhythmed blood
            is not your river. It's my river.
                        Boom
      and spin and shake through me. Divine
      shoulders move, and, sibilant, they cast
      off the fashioned boulder of this white
      crocodile. Blow. Bleach. A Nile hums
      my ill-fashioned marrow in this room.
            I am an unsavory lot of turn-
            toothed anglers in an oven-spring.
            This is not your glib neology.
      This is the whole room spun over me
            like a power outlet. It's the shell
                  that saves the whole
            wide stanza from dismay.

When I wake,   it must mean it is day.

Fox died lavender.   Italian

leather-look-alikes.   A borrowed thumb

smooths my hair in the oak picture frame's

sneer.   Most wood's heartless where I live;

   and what I wouldn't give for your couture;

and what I wouldn't shave to press my tongue

on your new-scraped tongue in your immense

                        bedroom.

           Our fog's like a fog that's dense.

Godiva

So sweetly arranged were they, my three
chocolates in a box, that I believed
them to betray magnetic north.
I thought they may have been celestial:
planets wrapped in paper, foil, clear
cellophane,   and every bit cerise.

I just couldn't eat them. I divined
a new arrangement for my furniture.
I saw shapes in their glaze.   I heard words,
and I ignored them willfully.   Sometimes
my great vision cooled and filled with fog.

I fed my chocolates to the little dog-
eyed face in my reflection. Showers calm
me sometimes. I turn red and my head burns.
I whisper to myself about autumn
and glob my lips with an expensive balm.

I believe in indiscriminate
wishing, and in omens. I collect
patterned fabrics. When a pattern breaks,
something sparkles somewhere. In the sky,
a tyrant lisps a list aloud and beams.

Oath

I don't need to know another word.
Sky-black, sky-black, handkerchief on back;
holly-berries, little printed feet,
lead me to the mead hall where I'll eat
custard 'til the sundown swallows me.
Ripe, untoward, and handfed, I am weak.
The earth could till me under quicker than
a lower row of lashes meets its mate.
Frost collected on a peacock ore
bust of you. I rambled to the store,
bought an amber six-pack to erase
my half-lidded image of your grace,
and grace, and saintly empathy.
What a patron you have been to me,
Endorsing all I am and all I do.

Mauerbauertraurigkeit

Let an oil spill of masculine
contentedness unstitch his cactus face.
He calculates the days on which he'll shave,
and feels he always looks best after two.
On the third day, he created rue.
You *cock*sucker,   he'd moan,   and I would pout,
and tiptoe to the corner with a trowel,
and bricks, and mortar,   and an inward howl
of pity for myself, clearly accursed.
He would gape grotesque; and, unaware,
would smear his glut-fat bear mitts through his hair.
I'd wear a basswood mask while I made eggs
and hiss sacred tobacco through a long
tube.   I'd draw four pictures of his skull,
entitle them: *North, South, East,* and *West.*
He'd know
nothing of the way he drew me close
in black, repulsive tantrums every day.

Act V

While he lies in a heap, the stars grouch.
　　　An exaltation stuns the living room,
Where, having vodka tonics two by two,
　　　He made a rebus of his love for you.
Pictures said it better. Things like doves
　　　Baked up on a nonstick cookie sheet. And sleet.
Nuclear little missives packed in small
　　　Drawings of dalmatians disemboweled.

While he shifts in his sleep, the night blows.
　　　Even tubers manage to sling blooms,
Even though they are most always white
　　　And easy: look how lazy Queen Anne's lace
Must be.　It didn't take a year to think of that
　　　Annoying saucer of a flower. And that smell?
While he mumbles to himself, the cabinets slam.
　　　Morning glories thin as dental dams

Dance over the east face of the house.
　　　Balled up like a spider on the couch,
He says he loves you like a coronet
　　　Of woodbine. Head: right, left; breaths: 1, 2, 3 . . .
He cuddles up in wooden misery
　　　And dreams of pill bugs on a marble plaque.
He draws how it must feel to rub your back,
　　　And warmth like butter breaks his tapered spine.

Before the Slow Dance

You ride into the red library.

Little quizzes vanish in your eyes.

Don't think your way around the red

fruit that glitters,   gyrates,

does not float.

There's calm over the terracotta path

that parts two curtains,   left and right.

Anger in your points   and in Calcutta

windows while the lilacs collapse twice.

Tiny vents and pinholes,   they are yours,

and you can breathe your glory from their map.

When you paw my screen,

and when you laugh

an earthquake underneath my stilted bed,

I quaver.

Some bright, wide absence

rings and rings and will not be condensed.

White hibiscus fades a wooden fence.

We loom above a sugared round of burl.

We tie our clammy hair back

in the mirror

an old credenza's glass has made for us.

Afterword

Hello nimbus, hello tiger-eyed
Dido. Did you get the dive down pat?
If you pump your arms and swoon like that,
over that escarpment, then you'll die
before the last adonic drips and splats.

I shove the olive under my pink tongue.
Imagine, the whole cemetery's ours
tonight while marijuana swads the stars,
and someone's old umbrella crowns the dump.
I lisp three *Vater Unsers*, then I jump.

Hello pavement-veined necropolis,
I come with seeds from England stuck between
my teeth, and burs from Hispaniola laced
like cameos throughout my rotten beard.
Who better to rub you than a bard

about to ride a lion through the dust?
The wake makes static ribbons of my hair;
I plunge to you from stories overhead.
Hello Congregation; Hell, O dread
Assembly of Dark-suited
Gentlemen.

The Suitor

I whispered glossy maxims through the ear
horn and stuffed my pockets full of coins.
Yellow orchids shone on the dark desk.
You were not seduced. I was a thief;
   my old linen sack was bottomless.
I stole off in my mint-green Cadillac,

glided fourteen miles from your house,
   then doubled back and analyzed my path.
      I should have driven farther, but to flee
         your cold, round, silver-plated hand
would whisper my head off and make me break.
I could have made you dumplings, but instead,
      I wore a knot of fennel wrapped in silk
and stuffed your mailbox full of sable crepe.

My Day Went

A knock at the back of the skull, *oh hello,*
a pleasure. I've blood sausage, mimosas, come in.
As they say, the brain, charmed, O resolute,
is warm tonight. An ancient miracle, what misers
do when it's early enough to be done.

A black-footed cat at the gate, my day went on,
alright. I thought about the kind of thought I prize:
the eye that takes the morning glory in
lately, mind that makes mosaics, mind that milks
the absolutist. For all that mind is worth,

plug-nickel knocked through the jukebox,
for all it fails: rising, the musical steam.
My dayroom in chemical distance, my energy rose
into my skull and unflowered its myriad barbs.
My day was an elegy always; my day had its charms.

About the Author

Greg Allendorf is originally from Cincinnati, Ohio. He holds graduate degrees from the University of Cincinnati and Purdue University. His poems have appeared in or are forthcoming from such journals as *Smartish Pace, Subtropics, The Portland Review, Narrative Northeast, Memorious,* and *The Hawaii Review.* He currently lives in Columbia, Missouri, where he is a Ph.D. candidate and Creative Writing Fellow at the University of Missouri–Columbia.

Credits

Author	Greg Allendorf
Editors	Kiki Petrosino, Ruthie Knox, and Mary Ann Rivers
Proofreader	Beaumont Hardy Editing
Cover Photography	Barbara Diener
Cover Design	Stray King Design
Interior Art	Ann O'Connell
Interior Design	Williams Writing, Editing & Design

Brain Mill Press would like to acknowledge the support of the following patrons:

Noelle Adams

Rhyll Biest

Katherine Bodsworth

Lea Franczak

Barry and Barbara Homrighaus

Kelly Lauer

Susan Lee

Sherri Marx

Aisling Murphy

Audra North

Molly O'Keefe

Virginia Parker

Cherri Porter

Erin Rathjen

Robin Drouin Tuch

CPSIA information can be obtained
at www.ICGtesting.com
Printed in the USA
LVHW091951091221
705747LV00008B/1609

9 781942 083221